AF817399

The Thing King

Other Books by Charles Edward Eaton

Poetry
The Bright Plain
The Shadow of the Swimmer
The Greenhouse in the Garden
Countermoves
On the Edge of the Knife
The Man in the Green Chair
Colophon of the Rover

Short Stories
Write Me from Rio
The Girl from Ipanema
The Case of the Missing Photographs

Critical Biography
Karl Knaths: Five Decades of Painting

The Thing King

Charles Edward Eaton

CORNWALL BOOKS

New York • Cornwall Books • London

© 1983 by Rosemont Publishing and Printing Corporation

Cornwall Books
4 Cornwall Drive
East Brunswick, NJ 08816

Cornwall Books
27 Chancery Lane
London WC2A 1NF, England

Cornwall Books
Toronto M5E 1A7, Canada

Library of Congress Cataloging in Publication Data

Eaton, Charles Edward
The thing king.

I. Title.
PS3509.A818T5 811′.54 81-70134
ISBN 0-8453-4743-8 AACR2

Printed in the United States of America

To Isabel

Contents

Acknowledgments

Agni Review for permission to reprint "Idyll of Isolato."
Antioch Review: "The Circular Staircase."
Bennington Review: "Debauch of the Chauvinist" and "World without End: A Japanese Screen."
The Centennial Review: "The Diapason."
Chicago Tribune (Sunday magazine): "Duck Blind."
College English: "Praying Mantis," "Mackerel," and "The Hanging Gardens."
Concerning Poetry: "The Avocado Connection," "El Dorado," and "The Muscle."
Confrontation: "Rose-colored Glasses" and "The Kiss."
Hawaii Review: "Exhibition of Blue Ladies" and "The Man from Buena Vista."
The Hollins Critic: "Paracelsus in Puerto Rico" and "Haruspex of the Happy Country."
The Kenyon Review: "Sentimental Education," "The Woman in Black," and "The Thing King."
Malahat Review (Canada): "The Raid."
Massachusetts Review: "Needlepoint in Autumn."
Modern Poetry Studies: "A Day in the Life of a Magpie."
Midwest Quarterly: "Don Juan in Autumn" and "Suit of Lights."
Northwest Review: "Artists Anonymous."
Poetry Now: "White Clown" and "Sumptuous Siesta."
Prairie Schooner: "A Dream from Hokusai."
Salmagundi: "Bodies of Water," "Articulation of the Ruby Bracelet," and "The Gestalt."

Southern Humanities Review: "The Paperweight," "In Search of the Sunbather as a Very Safe Thing," and "Purple Lilacs, Blue Water."

Southern Poetry Review: "Sleeping Nude," "The Amputee," and "The Blue Pajamas."

The Southern Review: "View from a Balloon" and "The Courtship."

The South Carolina Review: "The Palm Voyeur."

Yale Literary Magazine: "Bonsai" and "Duck Blind."

Acknowledgments are also due to the following magazines for permission to reprint one or more poems: *Arizona Quarterly, Arts International, Chelsea, Colorado Quarterly, Contact II, Dalhousie Review* (Canada), *De Kalb Literary Arts Journal, Discourse, Forum* (University of Houston), *Four Quarters, Harvard Advocate, Hiram Poetry Review, Kansas Quarterly, Louisville Review, Paintbrush, Poem, Poets On, Quarry West, Quartet, The Smith, Southwest Review,* and *Striver's Row.*

Also, "Purple Lilacs, Blue Water," "Duck Blind," and "Mackerel" were reprinted in *Karl Knaths: Five Decades of Painting* (International Exhibitions Foundation, Washington, D.C., 1973).

"Sentimental Education," published in *The Kenyon Review,* was a prizewinner in the 1980 Arvon Foundation International Poetry Competition (London), and reprinted in the foundation's *1980 Anthology,* ed. Ted Hughes and Seamus Heaney (Todmorden, England: Kilnhurst Publishing Company, 1982).

The Thing King

I *Messages from Metamorphosis*

In the Garden of the Fire Plants

After some talk of what is called the "realities,"
The man lit a match and smoked contemplatively:
All day, at intervals, these blooms at the end of a cigarette.

In the white soil of his fingers they were like wind-blown tulips
cupped and tipped in blue;
There would be a field of them in memory when curtains
closed for the night,
Now a bit like poppies among lines of stretched-out
gravestones.

The fire in the grate would stress the larger floral note,
Clinkered in blue, with the black fingerprints of massive tulips,
A crematorium where ghosts seem to escape from the open
oven.

One chunks the fire, and it leaps up, curls, folds into itself
Like the coppery yolk of an incandescent egg mixed with the
white;
The man feels as if a hot nebula were stirred in his heart.

Can one be much more organic with anyone than this?—
The white soil, the flowers, the spiral streaked in the egg,
The blue in the flame as though the sky's shell were cracked
into it.

Like the man beside the fire, I am always looking for a system
That can live by its own internal strength, that has no other
root
Than the hand that holds on almost to the point of burning.

But I have seen figures slumped in a room where the fire also
dozes,
The sensual mouth, a loose, depleted, full-blown tulip,
The limp white hand hanging down like a furrow.

All of this at the end of evening—a slag, a harvest:
The man stirs sleepily—one more cigarette, one more match;
The mind is a far-off mountain made of poppyseed.

In the morning, a great sense of debauch—cigarette butts,
ashes, dead bones in the grate—
One almost longs for an explosion when the pilot is lit:
That huge flower at last, lifted, shimmering, shimmering alone.

The Circular Staircase

It was like a screw pushed up through the house,
One more turn and it would have reached the sky,
The paradisal blue that roofs keep out—
It has cut through its store of opinions,
Thoughts, and made this striking place for itself:
A sense of keen, slow, swirling motion stopped,
Steeped in a scent of rustling skirts, starched shirts,
The baffled, returned waterfall of feet,
The deodorant on the dog's urine,
A basin at the bottom of the steps—
Pausing at the recessed stained glass windows,
One thought one was looking through arteries,
The rich plaque of our stalled experience,

Colors from millions of swallowed pictures,
The tongue still quivering, streaked with pastel.
It cannot mean just Johnny on the stairs—
The twisted larva in a hard cocoon,
The brilliant, encrusted wraparound—
It is the snake lifted in every house:
The old straight staircase wanting to squirm,
Urged on from below by an auger.
At some point, in any house, this image
As if a heartworm hid in the woodwork:
A man can start the gimlet with a kiss,
The gulped wine revolves in the pink gullet,
Women pierced by their lovers fall and fall—
Therefore, when you must pause on the landing,
Look up, look down, alive in the turned thing,
Your white hand butterflied by a window,
The throbbing spiral reaming through the dark.

Bodies of Water

Could he stretch a dab of blue, one drop, into a brilliant
  pool?—
He was a *tachiste* of some skill—so why not try it?
He could always be his own barbarian, having gone to Savage
  School.

But any man intent on making up a shining lake
Must find a hole in the world, the universe itself,
As if the master of assiduous texture were somewhere on a
  coffee break.

Perhaps for quite a while conceal the liquid in the mouth—
One must grow heavy, nervous as a man with prostate trouble
Who believes the blue in his bladder is an urgent power needed
  in a drouth.

Suddenly, the world looks seamless, solid, paved with hate:
That is the moment when the sleek barbarian will relieve
  himself—
Out of his body and his bulging cheeks the full-expectorate.

Ah, the relief—the brilliant, brilliant, brilliant blue!
He was prevented, and surmounted all perishable prevention:
There is a landmark on the land, personal, impersonal, and
  entirely new.

I do not need to name the selected spot, the unexpected pitted
  ground:
The rest macadamized, a battlefield of botches and
  dismemberments—
Systemized, succinctly powered, his blue can be, like murmurs
  in a ghetto, expansively profound.

The Palm Voyeur

Any way he traveled he confronted
The palm tree against a cloudless blue sky—
The lean, hard, horny trunk, the slashing crest,
The fronds like the backbones of great filleted fish
As if a monger's scraps hung on a pole.
Not a sign of corruption in the sky,
Not the least brocading of clouds or mist.
He tried to remember the old drugstores,
The ice-cream tropics, the large circular fans
Whirring overhead in stunted desire,
No color anywhere except upon the spoon,
This helicopter ghost not yet even dreamed.
But just that swallowed color made him rise
And settle in a land of sea and fruit—
And then to come unerring on a god—

The great green geyser of these flashing knives,
Strong enough as an Idea, a dasher
To turn a freezer of lime ice forever.
So much for the boy's drugstore fantasies,
One thing, but an important thing left out—
He had found his locus, latent weather.
But strangely flattened now, a lichen on the sky,
The palm demanded: what, of what, and why?
Search in your own concluded mind, voyeur.
Does a black beach boy climb the heartless trunk
In desperation toward a coconut,
Struck for his trouble, rich adoration,
By the heavy blind skull that holds the milk?
Think back as far as the moist, dark soda fountain.
How much did you know of what you really loved?
These stunted images rise and rise in us,
Powerful, simplified at last, and There.
Great and circular travelers that we are,
The eye, it seems, can only tattoo palms.

The Blood Buoy

It was quite simply and forcefully painted a savage red—
The blue of the sea was violence itself that day,
And the buoy bobbed in it like a bloody, tethered head.

Sometimes it takes just such a wink of color on the water
To make us reach up to the handsome herm we wear,
Grope, fondle, feel if there were any sanguine drop or
far-flung spatter.

Not much of any reminiscent feature there—
Just a brilliant head struck in blinding light—
How then does one conclude we make a rather archetypal pair?

Perhaps we share a tremor—just that, no more—
The lissom head can shine, vitally irrelevant as a lantern in the sun,
And still, like a hidden, bloodied thing, be quaking at its core.

We do not, cannot, pause for long—the buoy earns a passing glance,
But it flashes, pierces, and we keenly flash in turn,
Take note of how little footing here and there, and yet we cast a stunning lance.

Let me tell you it is one thing to see red, another to make and feel it enter—
The buoy nods an implacable blow to me, and I lash back:
We know, oh, yes we do, we blink and blind together, striking at the center.

Mixed Drinks

One must always be very rough with them,
Those images of goblets filled with rubies,
Imagine what it is to drink, be choked
With such sharp, glittering, crystallized wine,
Or jostle them and spill out the red dice,
Playing for a piece of the blood country.
You must be ready with your own true blush,
Not the flush of alcohol, nor the mere
Quick acquisitive grasp of these chance gains—
You have your own natural thirst for rubies
Just as those looking at peacock feathers
Make inlets in their entrails for the sea,
The flotilla of eyes, the gloss, the sheen!
Someone under palmettos in the sun
Wants only orange peel, the sea's thick debris,

Having sucked sapphire till it turned to salt.
So one must have a way with potables,
A tough, tempered tongue for liquefaction,
Such vast expertise with silt and clinkers—
I have seen these men under awnings
Studying their drinks, clear, opaque, and beaded,
As if all their colors contained a mood,
Some something they may have done with their lives
Or mean to do with just one more deep draft,
Gripped, glowing there, the pitiless, poured thing.
It is so intense, one feels the jewels
Melting, the peacock eyes leaching the tide.
That is why one calls on rudeness and strength,
Beneath the awning, the fierce, hooded face—
Keen as Eskimos displaced, to look out
From the parka on a land without snow.

Red Snapper

One wants a blue shadow underneath the plate
To know that the red snapper lived unconsciously in the sea
And never for one moment intended to be the thing we ate.

His blue environs must have seemed to him so vast
That the shadow of the passing boat was just a larger fish—
What infinitude of water ever predicates the sinewy arms that
cast?

Between the pot and the moment of extraction, the lofty vision
fails—
Lying on a bed of cooked vegetables, onions, tomatoes, peas,
He looks stuffed and stewed to running over with his own
entrails.

Then finally the extension of it all, the serving piece—
The sinewy arms are folded still, but the mouth must salivate
Until the syllogistic end: I am, I was, I cease.

Therefore, we simply must have it, it is not at all too much:
That bit of coercive blue stretched beneath the plate
As if some apprehensive student of Boudin put in a painter's
  touch.

What the absorbed fish believed in, we must too—
It floats the remains of the snapper on a brilliant catafalque
As if there were much virtue in this confidence in blue.

The Winch

The man lay among fallen qualities,
Rich, sunflower-colored stone upon him,
Broken bottles of wine spreading their blood,
A heavy, white statue kissing his mouth,
The linen suit close as a winding cloth—
What happened? He remembered the view to the sea,
Lunch al fresco with a beautiful woman,
The wine in the cups like purple tulips,
The leonine face of the wall fountain,
And then the yellow wall leaned over them
As if they had had enough of this world—
Breaking the crystal stems of the flowers,
Putting that plum in her mouth like a stopper,
Shoving him at once into stone embrace,
His soul in the foot with the broken arch.
No one who has not had a perfect day
Can lie so powerfully beneath it.
Who would have known the sun had a spike in it,

Shafting in a long glimmer on his chest,
That her perfume concealed a dungeon's breath,
And the blue sea crooned its mythical lies?
Well, the watch is broken, but the gold chain
Offers its absurd chances to his body,
The fob repentant as the wrecking ball.
At the end of the loveliest fallen day,
Listen to your slender residuals:
The slightest shifting of the French-kissing head,
The unscathed plum, perhaps a whiff of perfume,
Your good foot tapping the stone for a key,
A toppled rose trellis offering transfusion—
The foot gets out of its shoe and turns;
One hears, one thinks, a faint, far-off, *je t'aime*;
The chain goes tight as sex in the darkness—
How did you hide and hide these deep arcades?—
The next time you give yourself to pleasure,
Lift your hand a little to the wheel,
Whetting it with the pressure of your lips,
Advising slow motion to hand and plum,
Blowing, oh so gently, on those tulips,
Glad to have the watchchain dangling from your vest—
The sea tells lovely and truthful stories
When we lift the handsome liar in our midst.

Paracelsus in Puerto Rico

The young man looked and felt the gold on muscles was
  applied—
Under the flamboyante tree he stood naked and nothing
  mattered
For nothing like his golden figure ever died.

There were means and means—golden means—never ends—
The large red blossoms falling copiously from those wide boughs
Had fire in them but not a spark for pyres since he and such bright flame were friends.

Let me picture that flambeau. The flaming, unignitable, gold youth—
Gold teeth, gold plates, gold-headed canes come later:
The suttee, in the smoke of centuries, seldom is an early form of truth.

I sometimes spend some time at night, the leaden hour,
Using just what heavy metal I can spare
Alchemizing, alchemizing the slow-debasing lineaments of power.

It was so still beneath the tree except for red, so red, those fatuous tears—
I can smell the heat and scent beneath the golden arm,
See the legs he spread apart like long, exact, decisive shears.

One does not want a blanket—when red is corpulent it is much too red—
One asked for nakedness without a sense of nadir,
A figure standing in a fountain of red fire, if perhaps a bit alloyed, not yet detected.

The Paperweight

This crystal eye with a pink rose in it
Comes all the way to us from David's stone—
Just holding it, a curious sense of socket,
Tactile memory of the giant's body.

One's own eyes seem all too jellied, soft:
Here, the weapon extracted forever.
Some soldiers cut rings from fingers, pull gold teeth—
David knew much better, and took the eye.

It must have been cloudy indeed at first,
A kind of heavy, bleak, dimmed-over egg,
The huge, powerful, clear overview lost,
The insouciant seeing to the world's end.

Now that it has cleared again, sits firmly
On the world's affairs, it can well afford
The conceit, absurd, enchanting—the rose
As the pink pupil of a pachyderm.

I roll the eye in a dry, clean hand,
Love its frank, meticulous savagery,
The pressure of circumstance to which exposed,
The way it magnifies a check's signature.

And yet somehow one wants to fling it back,
Drawing a rainbow of filaments with it,
An incredible extraction much as
We used to pull a tooth with slamming doors.

One wants to let it fall, fall through darkness:
Meteoric, brushed, but not reductive,
An eye forever looking for a face—
A place of vision like a shining lake.

Haruspex of the Happy Country

This is the luxurious and exquisite land where all can cope—
Let Sisyphus have the boulders, stones, the steepest hills:
Here fierce ambition cannot have its way with those rolling
  oranges up a gentle slope.

We have had the open sea, and now prefer lagoon
So blue the swimmers want to dye their skin—
"Blue Bathers"—as if all their art would start a movement soon.

Which is not to say that now we have accomplished every wish,
But, having broken more heads than coconuts, we would
  extract the milk,
And having dived and dived, we dive again—this time white
  teeth bring up a gleaming fish.

In this land where absolutely nothing fails,
We feed the sloe-eyed girls pitted dates and apricots—
How wise they are to come to us, dressed only in a waterfall's
  prismatic veils.

It is not that you are innocent, young,—*au contraire,* you are
  much older—
From blue bathers you have learned a tone, a temperament,
And no dodger is more artful than the one who has retired
  from pushing up a boulder.

You are a man who can discover countries, sitting in an easy
  chair;
Smoke a cigarette, light tribal fires, spread out blue entrails in
  the dusk,
And say: I know it is not here, but in a moment I can put my
  finger on it there.

II Lady Charisma

Sentimental Education

The man and woman went down to the green canoe
To make their fateful incision upon the blue water,
Steadying each other, when they entered, as upon a totally
   uncertain concept.

They seemed to be standing upon the vast, illimitable jelly of
   their desires—
The quaking of the water had, in fact, a certain comfort in it,
The solidity of their bodies swaying in a soft, primordial
   laissez-faire.

Not until she sat down in the bow and he took the oar,
She in a white dress and he in shirtsleeves and straw summer
   hat,
Did the luxurious, visceral shimmying reach its partial
   diminuendo.

Then they prepared to do, what we all must do—close the
   metaphor.
Perhaps they went to an island to picnic from a basket she had
   brought,
Perhaps the shadow of a huge tree would pallet their embrace.

He left the seal of his shoe upon the bank, she looked back
somewhat wistfully
As if somewhere there were a room with closely drawn white
curtains, a shaded lamp,
Two contented people doing nothing more demanding than
reading books.

I thought of this fabulous duo just this morning, remembering
How I used to plush my feet in the mud as a child like an
unfastidious pigmy
To whom the apple-green earth was coated and cored with
sensual glamor.

The canoe painted with fruit-color slipped into the cove I do
not know just when,
Nor when the blue water came up voluptuously around my
muddy ankles
And I invented man and woman to step with some precision on
the rocking earth.

To this day I cannot dream these powerful, swaying figures
without frisson,
Wishing even to be a little godlike when I wake upon a dark
bed of jelly,
Feeling the cool breast of that woman in my brown, seignorial
hand.

I have encapsulated this vision in many closely shuttered
rooms,
Among bibliophiles, chez nous, silently, inwardly shaking with
inordinate passion,
Letting the keel of the green canoe cut the pages, white, so white,
then blue.

Lady Charisma

The woman wanted iris to pierce her,
The lovely woman with her modern void,
This dark woman, a target without eye—
In the bright streets or in the living room,
She would pause, stand, as if to say: Take aim—
Anyone, everyone, the world, at once,
This huge, in-pointed rushing of purple.
It was, she said, her iris feeling
Such as she saw the flowers in the morning,
Pointed, incredibly banked, against her.
She could be drawn to a man by something
As subtle as an amethyst stickpin,
An eye with violet tones her picador.
She was ready for extreme theater,
Her eyeshadow lifting a deep curtain,
The long view to the backdrop of mountains.
You have seen these women twisting blue beads,
Hung in a noose until they break and spread,
White as a corpse among the little buoys—
A pen dipped in blue ink and you may be safe:
Give a lifeline to an iris woman,
But slowly, calligraphic of the sea.
Put some kind of drag on the huge bouquet,
Feed her the blue world as it should be fed,
Infinitely heaped, hooked along the line
As if the loose void needs repeated tacking,
Pulling her while she thinks that she pulls you,
A shower of beads, a stickpin in the heart.
Who is the authority, the one in charge?
The orator of ink asks, idling a conclusion—
Even the sea runs back to its shadow—
Write a canto on the long, loose float
About immense moments of living jewel,
Two dripping figures losing purple sweat:
The lassoed woman and the iris man.

Praying Mantis

One dreams these insects in the sun, their legs like knives,
Puts a hand to the chest to see if it is male and armored,
Hallucinates a bit jilted girl friends and abandoned wives.

This is what can happen to the disappointed lover—
Here in the sun, as if he quivered on a leaf,
Massaging for the soft spot, he feels himself all over.

It is absurd to say to oneself on this bright day
That any woman could come forward with her white arms
  lifted,
Intending to devour him though she pretends to pray.

He can almost feel the jaws on his cheek when she says, "Dear,"
As he has done so many times and brought her to her knees—
Someone always wears the solid plates of joy, and leaves the
  bitten ones of fear.

Like many, he is one of those who never could quite blend
What he has done to others and what they have done to him:
Mantis religiosa, worlds of love indeed, world without end.

Therefore, all these praying beautiful women, green and white,
Must simulate for him their lethal meal a day,
Show themselves full of what he is not—too wrong for prayer,
  for love too right.

Steps Taken in a Debris of Day Lilies

These brilliant flowers look sent from the sun,
With the same pulse as the light that lasts forever,
Yellow, sunshine-heavy, streaked with topaz,
That jewel-hint of the burden of time—
The woman, too, like a lily in the sun,
In her green dress and coil of yellow hair,
Rich as a hive, honeycombed with amber,
Has a pulse that is the same as sunlight:
The soft beating in the air, the flower, the flesh,
The large drum in the sky, the little drums,
The muffled gong-sound and the counting ear.
The woman stands, steeped, a little heavy—
What is one to do with the soft burden
Of life, veined, secretly lined with topaz?—
Merely let it delta and leave its brown lode?—
The sunglasses warming the brain-water,
A necklace like a river amulet,
On the fingers, the residual rings?
The woman moves, the flower, the light, exhale;
She takes a breath and draws them back again—
So there it is—this longing to beat the drum,
The wanting to be a pure dynamo,
This putting a dam across the river,
Yet heavy, silting, the soft pulse inlaid—
The rates go up for a day in the sun:
A finger and then a hand of topaz—
At night under the soft yellow lampshade,
Like a turned down lily, ready to drop,
The woman sheds her pollinated jewels,
Reads a story about the sun's far death:
If someone is trying to frighten her,
She will turn out the light, lift up the lamp.
It is still warm by the river—You can
Hear the lilies feeding on the starlight.

The Philtre

The man was feeling dark, not midnight-blue, but almost black
of late:
A trace of hemlock here, a trace of hemlock there, some vice,
some void,
And not any of those exquisite girls-cum-courtesan who used to
mix the mithridate.

One day the last of them came by to say good-bye—
The whole sparkling world had been their drinking goblet:
Was it really time to stir the final pellet in and put a lid upon
the sky?

At first she seemed to hesitate, to want to be his former pet,
And hid the secret dosage, so much darker now,
As if her lovely hand concealed just a bit of violet.

Violet hours will do, my friend, when we have spent the golden
ones—
She said this with her kiss which even tasted of the flower,
And kept the tincture for the last—the one distilled from
setting suns.

It was as if she quietly dropped into his drink the essence of a
deed,
Or many deeds. Why had he not seen her calmly stringing
them,
Keeping back for final, unsuspected flavor the one dissoluble,
jet bead?

I contemplate the man, I drink his potion, when some lovely
creature turns her back,
Goes to the kitchen, so she says, just to pour another drink:
I remember all the little things, and see the liquid, golden light
around me—oh, so subtly—turning black.

In Search of the Sunbather as a Very Safe Thing

There was no need to shake the idea-bank—
The girl was a stunning figure of gold,
Not one to be bought with pennies for her thoughts.
Since you cannot own a reclining element,
A less commercial approach must do:
Borrow a deep blue sigh from the pool perhaps,
Think of the brilliant light as a mirror,
Deft, offhand, oblique as Perseus.
But the old money-theme keeps coming back,
The desire to squander mentality
In the hard, absolute purchase of life.
Say what you will, we corner, collect,
Say no to reproductions, figurines.
Still, we will forever hide the miser,
Despise him a little, go on looking,
Knowing warm skin has a touch of the ingot—
On past middle age, keeping our thick coins,
Guarding the jackpot in us, swelling the till.
But the girl, sensing our metallic dreams,
Rises, miraculous without gold dust,
The crown of hair crumpling in noiseless
Dive into the pool, folding like a banknote.
You have seen old men throw away their money,
Jingling their pockets for odd, hopeless change.
Ah, say, ah, says the pool as the girl swoons
Down into some loose, large, Egyptian depth—
We hold out for the hankered, heavier thing,
Harboring the wish that gold can really float.

Articulation of the Ruby Bracelet

It was as though she had found the secret
Of his warm veins in the jeweler's tray,
Selected, with the instinct of a vampire,
What he might have given to a blood bank.
She knew he had never been bled before
By the way he paused, went a little white,
Then saw in an instant she would not settle
For less than maximum saturation.

It was the last thing she took off at night,
The stretched red tongue lying on her table,
Something to be stroked for its hard language
When he lay mute and wordless beside her,
Having left red-stained footprints in the dark—
He would go to sleep stuck to her sharp kiss,
The cherished bracelet in chromatic throes,
Unfondled, a jeweler's idiot after all.

One wonders what, in fact, it said to her
All night in her incomparable deep sleep—
That she had a source of life near at hand?
It may be significant that when she died
She was buried in the glistening bracelet.
One hazards these things—but the man lived on,
Healed, impacted now, rubies to the hilt:
No one could make a language out of him.

The Raid

The lovers had laughed, played, and grappled like sister and
  brother,
Pulling at plums, pears, nests, hives of honey.
Each was like an orchard to the other.

It was delicious, delirious, it ran with juice—
Two supple figures that would not be stolid, would not stay
  put:
The smallest white grape of an earlobe had its use.

People speak of the gray world, the world in black and white,
And relegate to some archaic dream this sportive pair
Who appropriate with no small grace morning and evening
  light.

Ironies, of course, begin within the clutch
Unless they do not look around them in the world at all
And do not sense some fading ground beneath their
  shimmering touch.

Plums do lose their blush, and pears do fall—
Sense how the cities creep and settle round this notion:
The boy suits up, the girl accepts the moment as ephemeral.

Those rolling bodies in the orchard glimmer like a toy.
The light grows old indeed, but in that childlike, yearning way
Of men who draw the shades at night and make their forays in
  the guise of some ripe girl or boy.

Sleeping Nude

The nude looks shot with tranquillizing gun—
One could examine her body, tag her;
One could look at the teeth, lift an eyelid,
Close it before a drop of blue leaches out.
You could put a clip on one of her breasts
If you wanted to—she is that relaxed.
An owner's medal hung from her soft pearls
Would advise her where to go when she wakes.

But the fantasy of strict possession
Lasts less than an instant inserted bromide.
She wakes at a sound, perhaps your odor
In the room, makes her own accurate shot.
You feel the stigma in your hunting clothes:
You must revive the animal, release it—
Some such shaft of alert understanding.
The man later made the nude his lover
And the grass was tall and lush in their lair.
Still they were aware of those roving hunters
With the tranquillizing guns, the labels.
He could see the woman transform herself
As shadow slouched like a brim on her face.
Her hair sometimes smelled of the iron of a gun—
They were in love for as long as they lived,
Not innocent, at peace—but powerful,
Observed, sleeping in tags, then poised for flight.

The Woman in Black

No one would have seen the garden as he did,
Heard the ululation, felt the violent throbbing,
Posed the beautiful woman there in the little nothing, in black.

To some just an egotist who wanted to anticipate
The sad cry in the garden when desire fades,
Who contrived well in advance, to see this figure so
understated as to suggest mourning.

He himself, with his black hair and white suit like a confined
Pierrot,
Nevertheless may remind us a bit of ourselves,
Those of us with our floral veins and our black nightmares.

I am speaking of men who have done it all the other way,
Loved the voluptuous, complaisant women in their brilliant silks,
Let the gardener alone dispose of the corpses of flowers.

But, suddenly, some time near sunset glow, the woman in black
Occurs as perhaps the only extension possible,
Suitably dressed for almost anything that could happen.

Will you let out your flowing sleeves, Pierrot, will you dance?—
The dark liquid in the dahlias still has a pulse,
The cry in the lilies is as coarse as trumpets.

One hesitates at this moment on behalf of the man,
Infolded onself, knowing what the trussed clown can do,
The absurd gyrations, the spotlight with the bloody dagger in it.

They are more common than you think, these women in black—the men with floral loins
Who look with such spoiled grandeur beyond the fading day,
While Pierrot is somewhere letting down the curtains of his arms.

Don Juan in Autumn

Fiery red, molten gold, but no leaf scorches—
This is a kind of sedentary fire
Which, for a moment, emulates desire:
The varicolored lover burns but not like immolation's human torches.

So, in autumn, leaves and lovers brood and brood:
How long can any flame remain impacted?
Have kisses held too long then overacted
And made the figure in the basement chilled and nude?

Art and architecture, fundamental founded—
The artful lover chooses just one word
Rather like a trill of fire he borrowed from a bird
Which will not shake the poise of cantilevers massively
extended.

The trick is don't go forward, don't go back—
Let the fires burn, but never let them flash:
The nude in the basement, clinkered, smeared with ash,
Attends the first exploding moment's bright, dispersive flak.

The Man Who Was Not

He was not a poet, painter, musician
Who are constantly engaged in *ave atque vale,*
But he had had his share of hail and farewell—

Of late, perhaps, preponderantly farewell,
A pulling away as from the back of a train,
A looking down from a peak climbed long ago:

The rush away and the slight vertigo of too certain
destination—
Let us, by all means, review the sensuous evidence:
For example, a woman he had kissed until he had kissed their
love away,

But not this clinging anxiety as they pulled apart,
Not this seeing her like a statue which had fallen into a ravine,
One arm flung up like a dropped, bunched, climber's rope.

He was the man all right who had loved her, so his driver's
license said.
Turning from that *fait accompli,* let us enter his vast collection
of still lifes
Where the incomparable peaches roll away from us like billiard
balls

And yet cache their pits in our pockets like an assortment of
red eyes,
Something an alpinist might find on his person and broadcast
to the wind.
Who stopped steeping the blue in the pool, who stopped
stoking the red geraniums?—

You suppose the man might ask, like a traveler evasive of
good-bye,
A sharp reminder to the standbys to protect the garden,
Pulling away, throwing down artificial rose petals if nothing
else.

One supposes and perhaps, finally, one supposes too much,
But in this woman's arms and eating the so estimable peach,
The motion of the train, the matter of the mountain, tell us no,
never, never—never too much.

III Among the Antipodeans

Bonsai

The man looked like a bonsai tree, squat and gnarled—
Life had cut him back, no doubt, over and over and over:
There is a stark pruning hand at work in almost every corner
of the world.

You know how it is when everyone believes
He can do more with your life than you can, cutting, shaping,
lopping,
Just when a lush viridescence puts out fresh branches and new
leaves.

Only the chosen few can have the full, glorious sun, some must
take the shade—
If you do not end up as a charming, stunted, maddening, little
shrub,
With luck you may be pushed against the wall, half a tree,
espaliered.

He has felt them clipping at the foliage and then his nerves—
There go the fabulous fountains of green, sheared by the
barber's hand,
All the phenomenal height of growth and its voluptuous
curves.

One may have a kind of strait, bizarre perfection as a stunted
thing:
The midget bird of paradise finds landing in its branches,
A whimsical wound-up toy of a lovebird clears its metal throat
to sing.

All well and good for some, the lawful, stringent hand,
But most of us are latent, lavish ones, our iridescence curbed,
  an aria suppressed,
Tense, telescoped within ourselves among the rocks adroitly
  placed, the little mannered heaps of sand.

The Kiosk

One would think he were sitting in a cage—
The man in the black suit, rigidly posed—
Or a thatched pigmy hut in the forest.
The sun makes those bright essential gestures,
Disposing in its way of all enclosures—
The huge trees murmur many things to him.
The man wears a death mask nevertheless,
Propped in his open-air mausoleum.
One must be hard, somewhat brutal sometimes,
And ask why one has placed the figure there,
Sad, sequestered, psychically loaded,
In the elegant little pavilion
Suggesting blue mould and moulting shadow.
Is this where all the clowns come home to die,
And moonlit Pierrot faces morning?
Remember it was a rich, lucid day
When you did this to yourself, depositing
The dark man in the brilliant summerhouse,
An exposed, absurd place of detention,
Almost like a stark lure for cannibals,
The fresh warm meat of life gone white and cold.
This makes the black spot on your lover's dress
Look like a disc more potent than the sun.
You may spend many convict hours there
Until you long for the spot remover,
A clear liquid to cleanse the leprous trees.

I tell you this with a mole on my hand,
Recuerdo of days that would not rub off.
Prop the figure on your bed, if must be,
Stuffed with glut of your own vivarium—
It is not fatal to Apollo types
To find the back one day less pliable,
Even the lover, Swiss-dotted, dark—
In fact, kiosks run a cleaning service:
All things, including spots before your eyes.

The Dining Room

It was so still in the room, filled with mirrors, men, women,
  flowers,
Touched with narcotic beauty. The old brain luxuriated: I have
  come to this,
I have arrived at an incomparable setting for my finest hours.

Born in the tropics, reared in the north, knowing too much
  rain and drouth,
I sit among these other seasoned and resourceful travelers,
Our old percussion dimmed to bringing silver to the mouth.

We have reached the ribbon, finished somehow in the race.
The woman opposite me must have run ten thousand miles—
No perspiration there: You will not see the massive mileage in
  her face.

We were, of course, making up our language all along the road
With only the vaguest fantasy, far off, of mirrors, flowers,
Where one could count on perfect translation that did not
  violate the code.

Why was the room so still then, so full of dying fall?—
The tables were centered with rigid masks of flowers;
Poured like blood into the glasses, wine was terminal—

I cannot say, except, speaking for the brain, one wanted far too much—
Look at that man, that woman, awake, dozing in the mirror,
While fate is running somewhere wildly on the road with just their vision as a crutch.

The Amputee

Sometimes it was an arm, a leg, a hand,
In throes, the head severed from the neck—
He lived among a world of floating parts
Which meant to roost on a style of their own:
The winged hand in a bed of blue iris,
The stalwart leg holding a sundial,
The head in a nest of pink impatiens,
One part at a time, saving adventures.
Some would love his hair, so let them have it,
His smile like curtains for a small theater,
An eye, a lavaliere on a warm breast,
A roving fetish, anywhere, anytime—
It always surprised him in the morning
To wake and find the heavy body whole.
Touch this, touch that, it must have gone somewhere;
The deflated socks suggest a journey,
The limp shirt, a white sail ripped from the mast,
This steeped, sexual smell in the warm skin.
Something, somewhere, achieved a life of its own
And came back happy, if a little used—
You run a body shop with these spare parts,
A loose inventory, a losing game
In a lush dream of some far assemblage.
A torso has gone perhaps to Paris;
The head preferred a lover in Capri.
In spite of our passion for diversion,
It is not easy to sit among amputees.
How long will it take for the lips to return;
The lost eye hovers but will not come home—
Why must we live like rubble in the sun?

The Cannibal

What did he feel when he bit into a luscious thigh—
Some premonition of sorrow, shame, some guilt, some loss?
What did he think when he smeared like large caviar the dark
  jelly of an eye?

Did he feel the liquid future smooth and rich as silk,
Running down his throat as if to nourish something other than
  his grossest nature
When he drank of the breast, that adorable, tender, and most
  lissom sac of milk?

One longs to know at what point he may have dimly
  understood
That of some things a little is much more than quite enough
And saw, like a world altering its essence, the victim he
  detached from food.

The most intimate and nearby would never again, by all odds,
  be the thing he ate.
The head that siphoned vigor like a melon felt reduced yet
  lustrous,
Hiding in a gelatinous pearl the power to discriminate.

Poor cannibal, who had to learn so many things from that
  deceptive day,
The doubts, the irritations, the psychic grain which makes us
  formulate,
The great, loose, lurid, meaty world filtered through the
  sobering film of gray.

He did not know how soft and stuffed with brilliance was the
  pearl—
The melon lies in the sun with languorous inviting limbs
  extended,
And in a moment volcanic with images, someone nearby is
  seen, dining on a girl.

Rose-colored Glasses

The blue eyes in the rose-colored glasses
Took on violet tones in that pink dusk
As if eyes could bring depths to rose windows,
Some kind of twilight stealing from the brain—
You have seen these women enter a room,
Their tinted lenses lowering the light,
Bringing in hints of dusk even at noon,
The first tremor of the sun going down.

Once you have this kind of installation
The subtlest of adjustments will begin:
The brightest place has the dimmed-over glow
Of a Viennese coffee shop perhaps,
Or the waiting room of a psychiatrist.
One wants a cup in hand, a magazine;
The shaded woman has driven us back
Into ourselves—we wait, we want feeding.

Should we pity the eyes which are enrosed,
Or does arrogance bloom in dark gardens?—
I met a great, rich sensualist once
Who said these women are the courtesans
Of sight—all drawn shades, shadows, and no shame.
One does think of couches covered with petals—
It is too late to be too ambitious:
We want a place the flesh has been before.

Purple Lilacs, Blue Water

Once a year it chooses you, this setting: purple lilacs, blue water.
Implacably, it designates the foreground figure
Whose back is turned, the face assumed to be a magnifying glass.

The other viewer, the one who saw the whole thing just a year ago,
Stands more than a mile away looking through a telescope:
The ocular exile knows the bliss of miniature.

Meanwhile, the face, as though it filtered sunlight on a paper,
Runs the risk of burning a black hole in blue
Or giving lilacs a brown preview of their death.

The town is full of just such last-time cases—
Their lives turn like the pages of a magazine singed in a brush-fire—
Ah, cisterns of blue water—Ah, lilac-scented bandages!

We will return to them with first aid in a moment.
Meanwhile, we are concerned with the implacable tension:
You must turn, walk toward the slow oncoming figure.

It is a duel—you magnify, he continually reduces.
People might come out from the town and park their cars to see the struggle—
Suddenly the gunmen seem to stop, turn their backs and fire.

So you can say it is a trauma—I have this dream once a year
Of inconclusive struggle; purple lilacs, blue water, burnt-out cases.
And you can say that I am more than richly endowed with fantasy.

So I give up to you the place of the foreground figure
And the ocular exile. This is one war no one should miss—
Though the guns are definitely loaded, I, for one, want no one
killed.

The Cork-lined Room

One may want brocade over it, of course,
As if cork, not wanting to be bruised,
Must be elegantly disguised, the hand
In a silk glove when the hammer comes down.

Morning's trumpet-sounds bouncing from the walls—
Violet evenings using their more subtle pick
Spot the white rug with amethyst chancres:
Could this illness be, in part, venereal?

The man observes the vulnerable windows
As if cloth were thrown over a lion's cage.
The shadows that come through are huge, pacing;
Headlights hallucinate their tiger's eyes.

Whatever the sensual variant you choose—
The den, hospital room, the lover's gîte,
Merely a place where the tooth aches no more—
You will want it inside-lined with living.

Believe me, the world's gullet sucks these cubes
As though coughdrops precede the sweetest kiss,
The tongue fondling, forcing seeds in the teeth,
As a snake looks for its lair in white stone.

Some may think it sounds like a coffin,
The body in many postures, poses,
But one would suggest the pincushion,
Heads keenly alert in pink labia.

No doubt a whole life of such lozenges
Counter-produces an irritated throat—
I have seen men fling open a window
As if exhaust were something like perfume.

Always then a pot in the cork-lined room,
A spittoon for those wads of gorgeous phlegm,
Behind a screen, of course, a toilet tic—
The walls can hear it, but the walls are mute.

Doctor Dionysus

When the X-ray went over his body
The search for the lost crater had begun
Along banks of the barium river—
Somewhere in his psyche there was a map,
But just try pulling it out with forceps—
Better these shadow-pictures back and forth
As if in fact they stroked a savage
With body-pictures of his own dark land.

One had never felt so full of flowing chalk:
Someone making notes with one's own liquid,
The staring anthropologist ready
To smear his face with war paint if he finds
The sleeping volcano, the totem cyst.
How can one be so tribal and so prone?—
One will want calamine upon his face for days,
Peering, remembering the intruder.

One insists—the strong, Hellenic sutures:
Sew up the dark continent forever,
The crater surfaces, islanded up, out,
Where twin Apollo swims naked with his friends.

Put down the pictures, kill the negatives,
Doctor, you cannot use that map again—
It would only take you to a painted sybil
Speaking from a mass of rotted dreams.

Fata Morgana

The woman born in island mist and fog felt that black
Was dominant—Even the sea, underneath, was blue-black ink;
The atrabilious crow came toward her, not just for corn, but
for attack.

The snake was glistening black with which she had to barter—
Other women had artificial rings and hoops of gold,
Or in the garden, as if for body's use, the supple, almost
suppliant green garter.

She recognized her plight as something one should never show,
But went to cocktail parties slinky, sheathed in black,
And tried to pass her theme around among the men as jet
seduction in an art nouveau.

Yet what she really wanted, concealed, but absolutely lethal in
her head
Was one immense, derisive but desiring jewel for her brain:
The showcase was all black, but the potent treasure was all red.

They will not rest until they find a man whose mind is like a
sapphire.
He must make up to them for fog, mist, when the sea was
black:
They will play upon his modulations, all in blue, as on a finely
tempered lyre.

They meet at bars, balls—the *bête noire,* the number opposite, of
course—
I have seen them standing, staring while the tender mixed the
drinks,
As if they saw, implacable, the legendary island figure rising
from its source.

Debauch of the Chauvinist

After the debauch, not one artery
Could quite remember the way to the heart.
What was it anyway—pumping station
In part, basin, a sewer for tired blood?

The last drink, the last mouthful of rich torte,
Seemed to have changed the old map forever.
There were Stop signs everywhere, and detours
Through ruddy soil always ended in impasse.

That dancer in the red shoes should have warned
Us, holding out the gemmed class of champagne,
Pointing to the staircase, the rooms upstairs,
The rapt fibrillations of tight embrace.

All the while the top hat smoked in the cloakroom
And the black cane grew rigid with waiting—
As you came down the brilliant marble stairs,
You were ready for any kind of prosthesis.

The white handkerchief where you wiped your lips
Bloomed with an admonitory, moist rose.
Somewhere a concealed clasp in evening clothes
Wanted to release its anginal grip.

Those murky backroads in the deep country
Need enlarged diamonds in their headlights—
All those lavalieres, those loose bracelets, rings:
How many women required for a lens?

I pause right here in the loaded blood's thick dream—
There are pistols, of course, if not old swords,
Underwear is clammy, smells of the swamp;
A toe escapes from a hole in the sock.

One rolls back in the mist a nursery scene—
Held in the diaper by a safety pin,
Harnessed, a soft, safe drop from a parachute,
You have come to the great circular land.

No wonder you go the rounds till circuits
Are grooved as close as phonograph records;
Women with red needles in their hands
Play you over and over, pouring wine.

One is always more impressed with the heart,
How it keeps its head, continues flashing sunrise
As if it tossed a red ball into the air
To go on bouncing over rushed music.

Even in the dark when the road is lost,
A little light glows, birds, flowers, float upward—
Somewhere a red fountain flows like champagne,
The women are waiting, slipper in hand.

IV Specimens for Psyche

The Manuscript Collection

So he would burn the juvenilia,
A little yellowed now, like old maps, charts,
But once stretched from a native's white skin,
The one who bronzed himself in the tropics
And lay under the jacaranda trees
With a lover while the trumpet-shaped flowers
Made a full orchestra of one blue note—
The sea suggested no harsh time sequence,
Just forever in her amorous arms,
The diapason echoing blue flowers—
Some hours later, behind jalousies,
Fingering the fruit brought in from the sun.
Why do the old accounts look dipped in urine
And smell as musty as Time's underarm,
Some of them still tied, forgotten captives?
Must one somehow make the day a blazing beach,
Give them the pyre, the suttee not taken
When the last blue flower fell, the wave dropped?—
Set by their ashes purple dahlias
In a vase—a respite from requiem?
One writes now, but for the old lush mistress
Who went inland with her purple garden,
Taking nothing but her veils, rich vellum,
Counting on lakes beside the house, laughter,
Some young man training in the strict gymnasium.
Will they even burn, those streaked documents
Soaked in pisspots?—coffins and coffins of them
In closets, attics, all over the world?—
I suspect it is much better to see
The stretched white figure of youth on the tomb
And let it go at that—No wise mistress
Hankers for funerals long before their time.

Exhibition of Blue Ladies

The tattooed lady had the blues as indelible and deep
As the etchings on her flesh. You cannot show the same
  pictures ad infinitum;
A gallery of skin has just so much space. You look and look,
  and go to sleep.

What does one do when one has been done and done all
  over?—
One cannot let the birds fly, the snakes crawl away, the rose
  wither:
You have an immense appetite for art—and this tight cover.

When was the last time you saw the needle flash, felt the thrill
  of being stuck,
Saw a virgin canvas hanging on an arm or thigh—
A brilliant masterpiece this time if nothing happened to your
  luck.

All those ecstasies—the life, the art, the bleeding!—
Nothing but déja vu in words and captions once so captivating
  there:
You would have to pay a gigolo to take a look at this light
  reading.

Well, call the service, negotiate the fee, have him come—
It is far better to have a handsome, pink, paid, young man
Than sit at home lamenting no more arabesques on breast and
  bum.

It is a blue life when we fill it in, *tout à fait*, complete, and do
  not try
To call in the world, even the bought world, to look the
  situation over
And find in pentimento some glorious stretch of skin that
  never met the eye.

The Gargoyle

The man was a lucid sort—The gargoyle
Never sat on his shoulders, never asked
That veins, a bloodline, be hooked up to it.
Still it sat on a perch somewhere nearby,
A kind of huge stone bird of memory
This bright athlete of quartz and comity
Might need when his whole life was considered—
A type of paperweight to keep it down.

Lives, even such clear ones, do fly about—
The paper comes up like wings around the hand;
Coats flap in the wind as if the body
Were a clothesline. Even this clear, hard nude
May find himself knocked about like a gold leaf—
One cannot always set down one's best thoughts
But sits naked at a desk where blue ink spills:
It wants an ocean off there, rough, somewhere.

I have dealt with these athletes at the table,
Refused their clips, little weights, marble hands.
Knowing how one must call for the gargoyle—
Even his shadow, and one lets down mass.
For you cannot be everywhere at once;
Even the light needs the heaviest seal—
Lovable, lucid men, what are gargoyles
Doing there but pressing faces on a coin?

White Clown

He has been dipped in desert dust at some white hour,
Rolled for his sins in the ash of cremated moths,
Or sifted like the dough of a figured cake with fine white flour.

The white is thickest, hardest, on his deadpan face
So totally matte the red-tipped nose gathers like a deadly
  fruit—
The lips, an outline of a red banana, still leach white as if deep
  down they know their place.

All white then, all given over, with just a touch of fruit,
The eyes heavily lashed large currants in red holes:
He is as perfected as the white foot of a dead man lying in a
  boot.

Our man of juice and sugar will do his best for us at night.
Every contrived thing we have ever dreamed of waits for the
  harsh day to be over,
And the spot that falls upon the clown is the heart
  surrendering its own implacable pure light.

Thank God, thank God indeed, the clown will never smile:
He is so august, arrogant, and at home with sorrow—
In this white country the red fruity smears are just the one
  barbaric touch of guile

He allows himself with children, white children, who
  malinger—
They must take back the light of their hearts, of course, in
  time,
All of them closing, closing, like a hand that hides a little blood
  upon a finger.

Butterfly Sheets

The blue sheets with the purple butterflies
Promised a vivid fantasy for sleep—
Just lie naked on a bed of soft wings
Like a white object on one of those trays

Brought back by tourists from South America—
No top sheet, pajamas, just the butterflies—
On warm nights one wants this great, soft brilliance,
A wandering off in exquisite luxury.
I give this lush fantasy on purpose
To an older man who has roamed the world
Longing to be tattooed in wing pattern,
Even willing to be pressed under glass
And glow like some monstrous tray in the sun—
Lying in bed, he is a colony
In flight, a thick swarm of iridescence.
Somewhere a huge waterfall thirsts for wings,
Drinking, being drunk, hung in the long grass—
The man cannot afford this ecstasy
Perhaps—white sheets, hard bed, the only touch
Of blue a cup where his teeth settle down
Like mouth coral, confined and calcified,
The lips bruised for a bird of paradise—
So I search among my lavish linens
Those that bear the heart's full flight in transfer,
Where the body worked its brightest batik.
I have heard the teeth rattle in the cup,
Thought what a mountain all our mouthings make—
That incredible peak of purple wings!—
Turned the night light on to calm the prowler,
Soaking his sorrow in a cup of blue.

The Haystack

Swains no more nor maidens, but still this place of rest,
This pushing one's face into the plump fiber of life,
This lying down along side of the Earth Mother and her single,
  mythical breast.

The arm no bigger than a white worm, the hand an etiolated
  bug,
And still these large, everlasting, grandiose ambitions,
This incautious and curvaceous lust to be the one to kiss and
  hug.

Yes, to kiss and kiss, and tell and tell—
The great fecund, feminine perfume that fills and gluts the
  throat and nose
Still conjures up the very day when Blue Man from the Blue
  Boy fell.

The dry wind whispers, and the hot sun makes him sweat—
Seeds shaken from his tangled hair propose: "Enjoy!",
And rich, compliant dreams of ravished maidens manage a
  "Forget."

No matter how long the amorous day may last, the stack stays
  big—
All the centuries, the metamorphoses, the transformations!—
It coils and coils its image round—a glamorous head of hair, a
  late, sophistic wig.

Ah, young man, modern, manic, you must go forward, beat the
  track,
Still pent, ejaculatory, arms tingling with remembered,
  tangential music—
Even a straw in the whispering wind, and Orpheus turns back.

A Dream from Hokusai

I lay on a mountain among the morning birds,
There were mists everywhere and I half expected
Old bearded men with Oriental faces
To rescue me, shouting foreign words—

The world divided yaws—Should one feel that much rejected?
I had carried my hoard to the topmost places:
Now it was up to the old men with lean dogs
To sniff me out and paw me over
Like ridiculous scholars searching for analogues
To the hidden, deluded, lost young lover—
I managed to stay still young in such an etching—
The quarry should not seem flea-bitten and old,
I must remain, at least by implication, fetching:
The unselected suitor in a story not yet told.
Suddenly I rose, a standing Buddha with my navel-calm
  exposed,
Bracelets and necklaces of mist shining in the sun,
And said: Old men, you have lost the way, you are confused—
And they looked up, lustful and young again in their
  consternation.

The Gestalt

The man lying on a field of poppies
In his straw hat, a crisp, spotless, white suit
Is a figure of dolce far niente—
Images of himself float through his mind:
Naked, wound up like the Discobolus,
Ready to throw away the day's burden—
That shimmering disc, that shiver, that fall,
The hammered, gleaming, expulsive body!—
Some oil then, the brilliant rubdown, massage,
Until the skin is soft as gold velvet;
A look in the mirror at the untrussed form
And he knows it is time for the white suit
Into which he can now be poured like cream
So rich it has a tinge of sunflower;
Then the leisurely stroll, looking for blood,
The bright carpet of spread-out contentment—

You do not project an image this far
Without naked flinging, oiling, buffing,
The choosing of the neat receptacle—
One has many choices in these matters,
The absolute *Einfühlung*—indeed
The invasion of a sequestered place—
Those of older hue may want violets,
The long sighing, the crushed significance,
The scent more bottled, less rich and far-flung—
But do not discount methods of fusion
When the scout of the scattered self,
Having on purpose broadcast its life, feels
A figure, in small revolution,
Resolving, among poppies, moments of peace.

Mackerel

This, my friends, my dearest friends, is the specific fish—
It hangs on a hook in an aura of gorgeous, pendent ornament,
The blood has gaudy, iridescent implications, the skin its own
  metallic flash.

The brilliant, blue-scaled sea, the fish, bedizened, interact—
I wanted a bit of the world to end when I hooked the fish—
Plain, blunt, salty—came up instead with this embroiled,
  embroidered fact.

Whenever we may take it on ourselves to terminate,
So much comes up clinging, draining color like a box of melted
  paints:
The body of the fish looks like the soiled, silver shirt of many
  things we did not know we ate.

Do not tell me then that I am frivolous or lewd
To see these ornaments as if the sky were now a shining wall—
I took my hardest, toughest chance, but could not kill, clean the fish, and so conclude.

You may see the richest image here—I hope you do, my dear, my dearest friend,
And never ask who owns the basic, unencumbered fish
Or why the decoration of the fact belies the spare desire to end.

The sea gives a little, but we, quite obviously, demand much more—
The slender, nervous line tumescent as an inner tube,
And the milked, gasping fish, spouting, overflowing with a rainbow in its core.

Duck Blind

Lavish every color on life and in the fall
It will have burned to ruddy essence in the mind,
And you will be there, standing in a duck blind,
Wary, but perfectly at home with the residual.

In so much thick, stalled, red and gold
Not yet resigned to ash and cinder,
You, the man of the moment, also tinder,
Might go up in flames if you are overbold.

Just then, cut from an Indian blanket,
The mallard rises and the gun goes off—
Too much by far is really not enough
To make a man of color quite forget.

The mallard rises, a bunched-up piece of wool—
The man who saw that cutout in the sky
Has just a moment, pondering why
The sun turns off, the woods are suddenly so cool.

Artists Anonymous

Healed by Mozart, I must engage in healing,
Move, like destiny across the creases of annihilation's palm,
Restore the health of citizens, educate their feeling.

This means intimate conversation, the study of causes.
I see the hope of song in the face of a sunflower perhaps,
I must remind someone to return here and recoup his losses,

Remind the gamekeeper, too, about the animals and birds,
We must not use them up. There should be sanctuaries
If for nothing but the refuge of exhausted words—

An Africa, yes, always, an Everglades, a swathe of sea
Like a blue bandage around a wounded mystery eternally
  convalescing,
Full evidence of replenishment, the malaise of liberty:

A tour of the grounds above all else to prove
How much we need as men, how much we need to give,
The stay-at-home and pilgrim passions of our love.

Leaders provide us "messages for our time," but here
We would employ the hand of the nurse who brightens,
  freshens,
And watches the pillow for the telltale tear.

Repentimento

Underneath the rich gold he could taste the brown,
This sometime chevalier of bitterness
Among autumn leaves with his glass of ale
As if his tongue knew how thin gold leaf was,
That he could lick a grove and not be gorged,
Touch lips to vermeil without a burn—
The taste of himself on a lacquered day.
I, too, have crumbled a leaf on my tongue
And read the braille of brown, see-through matrix,
The stripped, riddled wafers lying everywhere,
Snacks at the table where one drinks his brew.
Have I laved the bright world perhaps too long,
An old exquisite in a looted house
Licking a gold-framed picture overlooked?
The Canadian geese go cranking by,
Canny sellouts to the season that they are,
Increasing the threat of something underneath—
The foil falls everywhere and the fires burn,
Under the smile, the laugh, always something;
The lighted cigarette is a signal:
Off there somewhere, someone, something else.
One conceals, of course, pulls a loose gold hair,
Hopes it may be hidden in a locket.
What more can masters of fine finish know?—
Our chevalier, how can he be so blithe
Sitting in such repose of detritus?
One manages a stiff, archaic smile:
We do not mean to lose all overlay—
Leaves in the ale, upon the blackened tongue,
Report our kisses to the underworld.

V *Vivarium*

The Blue Pajamas

Color of faded blueberry, some strange blanched wine, the
wing of a bird—
I can still remember the nights I slept in those pajamas,
The incognito dreams, the singing words and wordless songs I
heard.

Of all the things we wear this always is the final one,
Intimate, poignant, pathetic, the most courageous garment—
We begin to feel its presence steal upon us like an emanation
from the setting sun.

No matter how many wars we win or what high purposes we
keep
There is the rendezvous in some absurd, implacable, stuffed
closet
Where, with secret voodoo, we salute the limp blue flag of
sleep.

My color, yours, but his, hers, may be flamingo-feathered pink,
The tawny tint milked from a tiger's violent stripes:
Pajamas have a way of looming there, like manifestoes, printed
with rollers of rare ink.

I stop flatly at this point, not wanting to conclude—
All day, vivid, in a brilliant ring of animals we roam,
And do not, until the ninth hour, to this great lying down
allude.

Then, wrapped in flags of a wine-moth's wings, like soldiers,
We turn, kick, sigh, moan, cry out in ecstasy and anger,
Banked round, in far-flung, broken rim, the town we could not
find whose blue fire smoulders.

The Kiss

Amid last night's clothes piled, hung, on a chair,
The night table's lackadaisical clutter,
I experienced an erection of language.
It was as though a large crate of lovers
Had been left overnight, nailed, unopened.
I must gather my concentration somehow,
The sunlight a lever—this huge upright
Carried up the stairs by the force of dreams.
You have had these powerful longings surely,
The unexpected weight deposited,
A curt demand for your forceful entry.
Coffee, cigarettes, then the screwdriver—
With great effort I can tell you how it was,
The nails dropping, the rough splintering boards:
I undressed at last the box of lovers,
We shared a stark deshabille together.
So I wanted a kiss to start the language-flow—
I am not flatly realist, surrealist,
But somewhere in between—I summon things.
I call to the morning gap constantly,
Deliveries at odd hours, redirected mail.
So send me a postcard of your latest love.
I do not need a kiss quite so heavy
Merely to share with you the great intrusion.
I have a garage attic full of crates:
One hates the clutter, keeps the same address.

Chocolate Cake

It came to me as a gift from a woman's hands, that chocolate
cake,
Fresh, rich, unlike those hostages to Pop art—
These were a painter's hands, I said, which somehow learned
to bake.

Chocolate, oh chocolate, the sweetest statement of excess—
The ripples on the icing spread from a massive tube,
And none would fault her if some had stuck in heavy,
hortatory spangles on her dress.

There are many ways of cleaning up after the extreme,
And she had somehow baked a startling lightness there,
No sand in the texture that spoke of boulders grated in a
dream.

I could go traveling anywhere with just the knowledge of those
hands—
There at the end of the road along with backaches and
boredom,
This powerfully capricious thing done up in swirling bands.

We need our lasting images and those that come and go—
I cannot carry slabs of stone through all my walking, waking
hours:
Eternal eidolons at the end of the day can fall and give the
heaviest blow.

I love the carved, grave, passionate figures of the mind,
But do not hesitate to set before them just this carefree,
calibrated, chocolate cake
To beguile, perhaps becalm, when all my prophets seem too
high, too heavy, or a little blind.

Red

Some summer days one wakes up wanting red—
From central casting of the appetite
A large geranium is glowing in the light,
A vivid spot upon the air where someone bled.

Beware of red petunias in a box—
Something sharp, ecstatic, happens to the eye,
A quiver in the brain, almost like a neural cry:
Am I this vulnerable to tribal shocks?

One reaches out to myths—Osiris, Isis—
We conjure up the red anemone
Worshiped, we are told, on bended knee
By those who hope to feel the death-wounds of Adonis.

But the power-complex holds us nearer home—
The brain stripped naked in a color-field
Does not need a single myth to yield
Its passions to the statuesque geranium.

Cold as marble—then the brilliant spatter—
Someone whom we thought was dead is rising from the floor
To take again the one wound more:
Adonis, Isis, and Osiris—All the poignant myths come later.

The Avocado Connection

Am I ripe, too ripe, and therefore liable to be bruised?—
I live in some of the same delusions as an alligator pear,
Too ready to be ready, anxious of status, or just a little used.

No wonder you catch me at the window staring at the pear.
It is a kind of little omphalos of curiously contained concern:
Am I a half so righteous egg as this, I ask, in some despair.

Does it militate against desire, mellow, or quietly rot—have I
  the right to know?—
I can stand with my best friends and feel in my brain the soft,
  black spots,
And say, there you go, there you go, you god-damned avocado.

I warn them all, just don't you come near me feeling for a place
  to mash—
I have sat in the sun too long, waiting, counting on the perfect
  time and texture,
And if I were you, with your big hands, I would not stoop to
  acting rash.

Illusion may find me here, mistake me for some green,
  ambiguous placebo, or a pill,
But I shall use every trick of light and love I know
To obfuscate, reverse the facts to read: rotten, almost ready,
  waiting still.

There are moments though—Good God that glorious sun!—
When I invite the sweet, demulcent, and divining hand
Which touches me to say: You're ripe, I know you are, you
  dear, you darling one.

Sumptuous Siesta

Preferably the shades should be half-drawn
As though the lids of the sun were slanted.
Then lie down without regard for others,
The prodigal son on a year-long tour.

The opulent bird you keep as a pet
May stay if you put a cloth on the cage,
Smothering his insults, profanities.
Since very few have canopied beds these days,
Billow a bizarre dream above your head—
But that comes later in the episode.

The incomparable trick is to be at home
In your father's house, always, everywhere.
Elaborate precautions are necessary;
Otherwise you find a zombie awake
And hogging the better side of the bed—
I am telling you: Be good to yourself
For twenty minutes. Take off everything,
Preconceptions and assumed attitudes;
Swallow symbiosis with the bird's tongue
Which can grow another and another.

Shoes, socks, underwear are the leaves and fruit
Of the voluptuous, disemburdened tree.
All I want to feel is the naked bough
Sprouting in a climate of my choosing.
I have merely brushed the subject for you—
Some may want a round mirror as voyeur,
An eye, but lovers often crowd—The door
Always opens on complete sophistication—
Those who take naps know that Lothario
Must be seen dreaming ever to be loved.

The Peacock in the Bed

One wishes to make a connection, say what no one yet has
  said—
Lying down, thinking about the world, a spreading radiance,
In less than a minute, one has a ravishing peacock in the bed.

It is like holding up the hand and looking at the sun:
The brilliance makes new plumage for the mind—
Is this then, you ask, something that no one yet has done?

Ah, how one needs, and longs for, the finest and most
  iridescent feather—
It begins in the mind, seizes on the hand, that skeleton of a
  white corpulent bird,
And takes the sunlight from the air and brings them brilliantly
  together.

It is better than sex, more of a copulation, that most rich and
  secret act,
When the invisible thought comes out into the world, insists on
  its appearance,
And floats the sun-drenched fan as if it were a primal fact.

I can withdraw the hand, shut out the sun, indeed, for the
  moment, forget the thought—
We can separate, make abysses, factions, fatalities in our
  moods,
But let the mind alert itself: With pinions, the hand is like a
  rara avis fraught.

Let go of it, let it dissolve again, eyes swimming everywhere,
  blue, yellow, green—
The world rests in us all—But call the peacock to the bed,
And fingers with their ganglia of gold, which never were
  before, have always been.

The Comb

The comb in her hand is like a brown wing
Remembering its whole life as it swoops down
Her hair, skimming the plump perch of her breasts—

Now that I have given you this odd figure,
See what you can do with it. I should say
The hair is thick as a stalled waterfall.
There is no scrap cartilage on the wing:
You must provide the brisk animation.

Addenda: the seated woman is nude.
There is a mirror like a silver vault;
Perhaps the bird's remains are buried there—
I have told you too much, I am compelled
To control the sudden, deft, concealed swoon.
So I leave you the inert assemblage.
You must take the wing, feed it a phantom,
Go down on your own the slick waterfall.

I come back into a room live with birds.
They perch on her eyelids, her lips and breasts.
The clipped, dismembered world is up in arms.
The woman who was the recipient
Later told me the story of her hair.
It did things to men. It enflamed their myths.
I had been right to leave and then return.

This is not a fable of pure freedom,
But of rests, intervals, restitutions—
I lend you my images for treatment.
The nude woman, of course, went on to say
That she welcomed me back with all her heart.
I became animator and stylist.
We had a very pleasant, long affair:
In the tact of absence, I earned my wings.

The Pointillist

Someone like you must live with cherries on his place,
Must want the scattered burden rich and sweet—
These latter days too few are eloquent of fruit, or state its case.

No other tree is quite so handsome-starred,
Tricked out by someone who has sewn fine hats and dresses,
Having bought, en bloc, a too abundant color by the yard.

Here comes the woman of the place and her attendant cat:
The cat purrs, she picks the cherries—a genre picture—
Is there a decorator in the world who would not give his soul
  for that?

So one must be the one who is not jaded yet—
Piqued by the milliner's touch and with an eye for art,
Someone like you achieves confluence of madame and
  maisonette.

There in the parted branches at the very top,
The woman, with her pupil lying in the grass,
Airs the red-hung studio a bit, then sets up shop.

Someone like you, some really brilliant chap,
Wants to be spattered, never to spurn, be spurned,
Catching pieces of a picture as he sits forever with a basket in
  his lap.

Slides

Tonight a sense of white sequins on the floor
Suggests the moon had an orgy in my room
Or I am a white man flaking enamel—
One comes home, stiff as an old urinal:
The chipped, beat-up places in lamplight,
A sense of sex and sorrow baldly fused,
This thick atmosphere of dirge and dancing—
One looks for the cracked white dipper to drink from.
I am implacable about one thing though,
Insisting forever upon a set of insets.
If you go back over the entire day
You can see white spots swimming in your eyes,
The napkin handled as if it were painted,
Eating only the plastic white of an egg,
Drinking glass after glass of cold bluejohn,
Your underwear developing arthritis.
Is there any wonder the moon intruded,
Tugging at folded garments in the drawers,
Waiting for the mannequin to come home,
Insisting on a little late roughhouse?
I have seen men often, known it myself,
Who lock the door, refuse to trip the slide,
Adept only at the closed and shut case.
It takes some pushing on the white-flaked floor,
But you can clear the moon and the madness out
With a transparency as bright as the sun.

The Non Sequiturs of Summer

At this late hour, in the waning summer, do not be afraid to
  speak—
I said this to a man who comes to the heaped-up fruit table,
Salutes the melon's bald, round head, brushes the nectarine's
  rouged cheek.

He might have been quite simply talking to his friends,
The high-domed philosophe, the not yet ravished, ravishing,
  soubrette,
And said to them as gently as he could: Yes, sir, yes,
  darling—summer ends.

I like to think before the season is quite broken,
Before we eat our words as we consume a glorious still life,
The man will find his friends are speaking just as much as he
  has spoken.

His hand laid on the melon's head is the melon's hand,
The crease in the nectarine articulate as lips,
And our benevolent bilinguist is not hard put to understand.

He will accept dictation as shadows of the afternoon disarm
The sun and take to writing flickering wedges on the wall:
Mene, mene, here, there, leprous on hand and lips in black
  cuneiform.

The man and I will surely leave the room before we smell
The wisdom in the head too ripe, the bloom upon the cheek
  too damp,
And say: We close our book of friends—not yet, not yet, the
  summer when the empire fell.

Needlepoint in Autumn

A gold wound but nevertheless a wound—
You know how laden late autumn is,
The morning sharp with bright metallic sun,
An early impalement as you walk the dog,
Up hill, morning meat, skewered by the light—
One can imagine the brain dividing the point,
A packet of fine stuck needles deployed
To complete ecstasy's acupuncture.
Step on a lost needle, I have been told,
And it can work its way up and kill you,
Embroidering the veins a little on its way,
The deep, secret, heavy lace of the blue gut:
There is an unmade afghan in us all—
The aim of an autumn day goes straight to the brain,
No long, uncertain, labyrinthine pull,
No having to pause like a metal fish
In the blood, hearing the heart's waterfall—
Once at the top, needles would rather die
Than go back home. They say to the grazed heart,
Rush on. The lithe stigma has reached its source—
I can look at old ladies with their crochet,
White as fishbones, a late, lucid, fine-worked man,
Stand by the wall almost like a hanging,
Clear in the knowledge of all the journeys:
I have been patterned in the ways of light.

VI The World Beyond

View from a Balloon

Once inside an image, stare back at life,
Accost it, encourage it to respond:
It must bring blood into the diamond,
To the garden, the warm muzzle of the beast—
The man in his blue egg of conception
Wants the sun to crack it with blinding light
When the beautiful sphere becomes too airless,
The blue flame in the icon gutters out.
You have seen a man step outside his thought
Expecting to be strafed, strapped, or strung up,
Regretting the niche and the domed blue glow,
His spit a drop of eggwhite in the wind,
An intraovum stickiness on hands—
Humpty Dumpty rallies, raises his blueprint
Like a call to the ovals of others
As if one rolled white marbles constantly.
You can hear them click against each other
In any gathering, cloudy, aping the egg.
One aggressive picks up an addled stone
And clears it with a brilliant, new picture
Which he enters, now ready to confront
The others, an agate metastasized—
This game goes on forever in such ways
That the world at last seems to be blowing bubbles:
Every face turned toward them like a spur,
A rainbow film on the poking finger,
The grounded icon swaddled in iridescence—
I have asked others how it was to float
An image—They entered without answering,
Pointing to an egg falling from the sky.

Suit of Lights

It is a room of white cushions, a pure white carpet on the floor,
Brilliant, complacent cockatoos in cages, and one late, lowering
savage,
Bleeding, and bleeding just for you, O picador.

You are the man whose strength is always in his luck—
This beautiful contained room will always be yours
As well as the man you might have been if you were stuck.

This is a proposition almost anyone who loves the sun
Can put to himself, the exquisite, tranquil house
And there on a luxurious carpet the tribal and subjected one.

One does not ride a festooned horse, of course, one does not
hold a lance,
No dung on the carpet, no acrid smell of sweat in the air,
Just this savage visitor, as if a matador did penance with his
pointed glance.

Thus I have seen the unharried, wholesome, happy few,
A patch in the eye perhaps from some bright bird's wing,
In just this way decide to stick their point of view.

The room will be brilliant, spotlessly white again—
Great aggrandizements of image may militate against this stain,
But time rustles the silk curtains—there he stands, in the tenor
of your life, opening another vein.

A Day in the Life of a Magpie

It was always there, the sea, the orange groves,
Cameoed at first, much smaller than Boudin,
The deep blue hidden inside the sapphire,
Hung oranges reduced like Indian heads
As if an oppression, a massacre,
Always preceded the landscape's largesse.
It happens almost casually at first,
A blue man rising naked in the mirror,
A real orange quartered on the breakfast dish:
These close, magnified, expansive figures
Filled with circulation, sacrificial acts,
The finger scalded alive in a cup of coffee,
The blue stickpin, a tombstone on the chest—
Things moving back and forth from large to small
As if viscera were fed seed-pearls
Once more as the day keeps threatening to close.
Whether it was when you tried to lance the jewel,
Or put lips to orange to blow some soul
Into it, I do not know, but the earth snaked
Out its long, glittering coast, the blue, the gold,
And offered once more a rescue mission—
You must pick up all the miniatures,
The burnt-orange shriveled heads that dropped and dropped,
The long, rusted blue nails which give lockjaw,
A Sterno can's sodden voluptuous fire,
Appraising the parts of that tight pavé—
Embossing, bedizening the driftwood,
These treasure troves piled high along the beach
May be the wick that glows inside the world.

An American Expressed

The man in the gorgeous blue dressing gown
Whose color might have been beaten from a peacock feather's eye
Was glad that it screamed a little at the world in this forced, strangled way.

How many peacock eyes does it take to conceive an Idea?—
Who drove them into the cruel, concentrated conception,
Who wanted to make the sky itself envious with such saturated hue?

I have sat quite naked in a room and felt the grip of that blue—
One can wish never to bruise the throat of a bird
And still know that the nerves thread themselves unwittingly with feathers.

The blue vein in the arm suggests a kind of beckoning;
One knows a hint of mayhem, crushing grapes;
The foot plushes down into the soft bodies of purple shadows.

Something is taking place in the paid-up, shuttered rooms;
Someone, obscurely known, leers from the revengeful, foreign mirrors;
A white skin secretly longs to be infinitely tapestried.

This may not be quite the robe for your particular journey,
But you will find your nerves as well laden with glimpses,
And put some other kind of flowing texture in your traveling case.

The thin, emaciated man looks very much out there, somewhere—
All this elegance in the desert or a land of savages:
The collapsible white body, the opulent wrinkled gown.

It takes some courage, traveling often as we do,
To hang out the garment which our naked hours wove:
A thread-end suggests the ravishment of unraveling.

Who would have thought we would lose so much weight—the
doubts and the dysentery?—
It feels hemmed with sapphire and burns a little as with
stardust:
One longs for the synthetic, throwaway cloth of less affluent
days.

Some one thing we can do—eat, eat again, then go—
The body swells a little to its former glamor with this naked
thrust—
The blue dressing gown, faithful as a flag, follows with those
letters forwarded from home.

The Diapason

Men become holy, naked in the sun,
Both ascetic and rich at the same time,
Their clothes crumpled in some poor horror,
The body adorned with these plain jewels,
The bosses of the chest, the intaglioed
Bellybutton, hiding visceral lustre—
This pale priest comes to us from Sybaris
With light instead of silk against his skin.
Lie in the international sun, my friends,
And let it talk to your clothes and exhort
Them to keep their peace a little longer.
Children crawl around like baby Buddhas,
The oil the lean athletes use smells like ghee,
A fat man sits for a study of Saki—
In this endless relief of bronze, the girls

Put a band around the middle of the earth.
Skewer the gymnosophist's mind—It turns
And drips like a golden shish kebab:
So much for the graven image in us all—
A drop of amber sweat scarabs the fly;
Clasped hands swallow each other like the brown
Snake that has shed its white exoskeleton.
Those who cannot writhe, wear the rough red spots
Of light's harsh, sometime hapless, harlequin
Which yearns for the autumn's solidago—
Otherwise, their unguent boxes full of alms,
Spread in a holy, clear hallucination,
Gymnosophists belly toward bronze mountains,
The mat of the map spreading like sun oil.

El Dorado

You will not find it unless you are extremely bold,
Cautious, wary, too, sanguine, stolid, hard-driving forever,
If need be, down to a skeleton, pushing across the world its
   heart of gold.

You see them hardy but unhelmeted where the traffic pours,
Glad that they can dangle just a precious thing or two,
But secretly wishing suit, shirt, socks would glimmer—
   throwbacks to conquistadors.

One must want more and more and more—some is not
   enough—
Until one can suppose oneself in the middle of the lake, a boat
   heaped with artifacts,
Like that priest rolled in honey and gold-dust, standing in the
   buff.

This is how a lust can reach a sorrow, going in and in, beneath the clothes—
One can become an uneasy god amid the earth's replete reflections,
And must sacrifice to oneself the very thing one chose.

Nevertheless, like all adventurers, we will finesse the situation if we can—
The cop holds up his hand, the loaded traffic stops,
Somewhere, far off, an almost sunken boat is rocking with that gold-enamored man.

So it was human, obsessed, neurotic, and never was a land—
Only a skeleton with a glistening heart can reach the Country of the Sacred Lake
Where someone richly dusted barks from that heaped boat: El Dorado—lend a hand!

Idyll of Isolato

Could he ever lose the notion of voyeur,
Not himself only, though he was surely that,
But the eye of the sun, the moon, the peach,
The blue pool in its socket of pure white?—
In him a narrower thing, the true peephole:
A finding of cameos everywhere,
Of jewels with their stabbing clarity,
An eye for an eye, a tooth for a tooth,
The going over the pores of the earth,
The pain in the eye pressed to the keyhole,
An enormous life groped by the nearsighted—
But, as every idea must be turned upon,
He will have a followed feeling always:
The brazen pupil of the sun at large,

The moon like the oldest face turned inward,
The amorous, rapacious, bloodshot fruit,
The blue dropped from the forehead of a god.
How can I tell you of this secret stealth,
Inch by inch, pore by pore, the going over?—
The skin knows that it is never alone,
The heart is massaged by a surgeon's hand,
You will undress forever in striptease,
Close white sheets know merely naked men—
Perhaps it is the only cure for loneliness:
Surely not to be looked on is to die.
I saw the man stepping in the blue iris,
Golden, ecstatic with visual stigmata,
Stirring the liquid for its blinding glance,
His heaped clothes holding pockets of mirrors.
He will catch, corral the multiple eye
One day, print its pictures in an album
That turns, as the seasons turn, forever.

The Hanging Gardens

The fruit flourished, flowers bloomed, the birds sang
All because the sweating slaves brought water up the hill:
It always takes these busy bodies down below to make the
gardens hang.

This said, and it has been said more than twice times over,
We do not carry sloshing buckets up without reward whatever
If, at the top of the slope, we catch glimpses of the lover.

Preening himself, sweet prince, he is a doll that we have
dressed—
The water of our bodies fed the peach he eats—
No hill, except for us, could wear a lavish crest.

This, the enigma always—here a prince, and there a pail—
You can change dynasties, adopt the demotic way of things:
Somehow, constantly equilibrating, this equation will not fail.

We lower, raise our buckets, and we sigh,
Search the odor of our skin for the attar of the prince,
And wonder, if, like dogs, we should let the hanging gardens
lie.

Something is right, of course, and something always very
wrong.
Homo fecit—Is the lover indistinctly glimpsed in fact a lover?—
Let fruit and flowers decide—let birdsong.

The Courtship

The man crashed into her porcelain life
With outsize shoes and enormous biceps,
A thick club to everything in the room,
Her nerves a set of Chinese glass chimes—
Some said he was a painter, poet, bum,
But, for her, nothing at all in a name.
Who else could have made a crude introduction
Stiffen her skin like enameled flowers?
Her instinct was to put up grids at once,
Lie in a nacreous place, protected.
But this man was a born oyster-shucker;
The pearl, any pearl, would lie in the net
Of his blue-veined hands, tipped by the knife.
Of course, she could kick him in the shinbones,
Make a fatal dive for his testicles,
Try jerking his hair, testing for root-strength—
At last the summer wind instructed her,
Rustling with ease the pendent ideographs:

When he had stroked the music down, the calm
Would enclose them like a huge, brilliant shell.
The man, however, had a different view—
The whole world is filled with our ancestors—
She lived in something clear, remote, lost,
He moved in a musk fog with large brass hands—
I have known them both, the husked, the husker,
Rolling my eyes in landscapes made of pearl.

World without End: A Japanese Screen

In and out, those mountains and those lakes,
The sinuous little yellow road the eye delights to follow—
How did the artist decide to pause, those breaks—in
  fact—non-breaks?

Most charming, that kimonoed figure with her puff of hair,
All splashed with color, her face painted like an everlasting
  doll,
Seems to know with such insouciance that she is gladly going
  somewhere.

Sans Souci!—I would put a mirror on my skin
And let my sloping belly play the mountain's role
If they would tell me, without telling, where I go and where
  I've been.

I love that little vivid woman, I wish like her to be reconciled,
To find the road both short and endless,
The land delivered half of opulence and half with child.

God help us—we ask and ask and ask for plot—
Why not? We feel ourselves entwined, ensnared, entrapped,
And cannot revel in the fact that woman there has deftly
  slipped the knot.

Denouement is not the language of the lake, the glade—
Yes, the woman has a parasol, unopened, absolute, so pink I
want its blush,
But sun is very clear and mild today. What lover's right have I
to say to her: Stop a moment in the shade.

The Muscle

In the mirror, the brown, bent arm reflects
A dune swelling underneath the tan—
What makes a natural desert in the room is man:
The muscle, like a brigand, states its sex.

You do not have to see the dark, burned face
To know the body had a love affair with sun,
Took the sweet seductions, one by one,
And brought them here to this sequestered place.

In such half-light the mounds of muscle shine—
Anyone who knows the brilliant body of the world, the map
Of where the tents of our adventures flap,
Can say that what the mirror harbors is not androgyne.

But then a beautiful white arm is raised—
Someone, voluptuous and pale,
Is holding up a dancing veil—
What was lucid in the mirror now looks crazed.

Every muscle in the world admits the risk—
It means, like Adam in his vigor,
To have the desert and the dancing figure,
The rigorous, mingled, mirror, and the odalisque.

Architectural Visions

The man sat under the weigela tree
In sunlight on the richest of days,
Under the curve of red tinted with purple,
At the heart of the stilled maroon fountain.
Now this strange man, no ordinary soul,
Had fallen beneath the wall of circumstance,
Solid-seeming, but poorly constructed—
Yes, it came tumbling down one clear day
As if an earthquake in himself produced it—
See now why he likes this brilliant stillness,
Sitting under the miraculous, saved tree
Which somehow survived the plunging wall—
One more sensualist, gone wrong, recovered,
You say, the quietus on the fountain—
You have a point there, but just a point:
The man is studying the situation,
His hand pumping the fiction of a jack,
At the plaza's edge of his own ruined world,
Not wanting the water to flow just yet,
The thick, close-bunched, bloodlike drops above him—
At rest, it seems, but intensely working,
The veins on his forehead, full, hydraulic—
Such are the lords of the great fallen day,
Just at the glittering edges of rubble,
Holding back the fountain now a moment—
Thus, the gripped jack works only in slow motion,
Faces, found objects, up into the air.
The day keeps falling, the hand keeps driving:
It is profound dreamwork now and forever—
I see these contained, bruised men, the leashed tree,
A clear, brilliant moment in the garden,
The great day wondering: When? What next? And how?

The Man from Buena Vista

Let us still reach out to what we most would have and be:
The man thought this on his terrace where he seemed
somewhat stalled—
Someone with a much more fluid net was bringing in the
islands and the sea.

Someone else was feeling the rich and lingering effects
Of purple asters in the garden, the smiles of beautiful women
With whom he had an understanding of the metamorphosis of
love from sex.

The wind on the terrace moved, but he had no oar, much less a
sail—
Just this complex vision of a statue and his name upon it,
Those fishermen with brilliant ways of taking in the world that
never fail.

Nevertheless, there goes the rigid hand plucking at an aster,
And when he has beautiful, understanding women in to dine,
He will set lanterns on the railing, alerting sailors to the
presence of a master.

Something may come of this exquisite meeting yet!—
Let them have their islands, perhaps the woman
murmurs—Here by a darkened sea,
The statuesque is flinging out its stasis like a net.

So we must tell ourselves as we unbend, bend down in
candlelight:
The woman brought up like a jeweled mermaid, the sea as rich
as wine—
Those for whom the day is somewhat over make their most
determined haul at night.

Portrait of a Man Rising in His Profession

The cherry tree floats against the blue sky,
White coral in a sea suffused with light.
Down under I am walking in my wet suit,
Wanting to climb the subaqueous tree.
Have I put too much weight upon my back,
Some enormous burden of fantasy
Heavy as a stash of old coins or a bag
Of sex plunged to the bottom of the sea?
I am indeed a prowler in the light,
Always rubbered up, the most literal
Of skin divers, weighted, unexpellable—
Does this in any way convey to you
The heavy and the drifting look of love?—
Light on my feet beneath the cherry tree,
The feeling that I must come up with coral,
The tree exquisitely silted in the brain,
A branched man at last spilled upon the deck,
Gasping the ordinary air of conquerors—
You know how the world gapes, fingers the loot,
A small, hard piece of calcium in their hands.
So let it go for this, yes, let it go—
The wavering white branches, blue water,
The man's submerged, resilient ballet,
The swoon as brilliant tree lifts up with him—
One rides the image as the season changes,
Guiding a cherry picker toward the sky.

The Thing King

The man had handled the subject of sea, sorrow, fruit,
  Freude—Geist—
He had meant to be one of the conquerors of life,
But something—Je ne sais quoi—had never quite sufficed.

He had treated the brilliant ocean like his own lagoon,
Eaten of every fruit there was before the Fall,
Sent all the pipers scattering away because he called the tune.

It was the words between the sea and fruit that clung—
The long, sometimes almost lissom, blue sorrow hanging like a
  limpet,
The joy, that should have spread its wings, too heavy for the
  tongue.

God knows his arrogance and pride deserve what they must
  get—
Still we bring him one more primal and preceptive fruit to
  taste,
And try to knock his coattails free of that suctorial blue limpet.

Therefore we take the words and give him luscious and
  lascivious things:
The sea that rushes in the grotto of the thighs,
The table where the mellow bottoms of the pears have sat and
  left their rings.

You bear the burden of depleted joy, I wear the lumpy jacket
  of the true—
No matter what they say about the death of heroes, down with
  an elite,
Without these loaded words to hamper him, the conqueror has
  other things to do.